Tattoo Apprentice

Sean Hobden

ISBN: 9798643596028

CONTENTS

Introduction

When I started tattooing almost 40 years ago it was almost impossible to get into the trade of tattooing, there were very few of us and tattooists were looked down upon by society so were naturally suspicious of newcomers. The tattoo suppliers back then were a complete secret, there was no internet and they didn't advertise so the only way to get hold of tattoo equipment was to break into a tattoo shop and steal it or more preferable but much harder win the trust of a tattooist to give or sell you an address of a tattoo supplier. There was no such thing as an apprenticeship for tattooing back then so all tattooists were self taught. Today anybody can be a tattooist but getting a job in a reputable tattoo shop is a different thing. This book is not for chancers who have no talent looking to get into the trade for a fast buck it is aimed at the people who have outstanding artistic talent who are looking at ways to present themselves to the trade.

Today the tattoo trade is saturated, extremely competitive and overcrowded but as the late Sailor Jerry said it's only overcrowded down the bottom there is plenty of room at the top!

I think in some ways tattooing is much harder than it used to be, it is extremely hard work and not for the faint hearted so it's only fair to tell you what to expect from a traditional tattoo apprenticeship. Traditionally a tattoo apprenticeship is a test of character as much as a learning experience. The test of character is necessary because you will be dealing with the public on a daily basis and although the vast majority of tattoo clients are lovely people some of the public can be very demanding to say the least.

 The first thing to do is swap the word apprentice for cleaner or even more accurate dogs body. For the first year or so you will not even hold a tattoo machine instead you will hold a broom, mop or polishing cloth and be expected to clean the shop, that means the floor, the ceiling, the shop front, all the glass, all the equipment, the toilets, the tattooists car and anything else that the tattooist can dream up. On top of this you will be expected to make the tea, get the staff lunch, run errands and any other chores required by the tattooist or staff. You will be expected to do all of this without complaint, nor should you complain because this is a valuable time in your apprenticeship to listen, watch and observe.

After this period if you haven't already left you will be given lessons on hygiene and cross contamination, stencil making, first aid, machine setup, tattoo positioning etc.

And if it's a street shop you are working in, answering the phone, the law and how to deal with under age kids, and maybe how to deal with drunk aggressive customers etc.

Then if you still haven't left by now the day finally comes when you are allowed to set up and hold a loaded tattoo machine. If you are lucky there will be a member of staff or a friend to do your first tattoo on, if not you will have to do it on yourself, this is very traditional, if you're not prepared to wear your own work for the rest of your life why should you expect a paying member of the public to do so.

At this point you are at the real start of your apprenticeship, congratulations you have done well to get this far and you have got through the worst part of the apprenticeship, paying your dues up front in the form of hard menial work. At this point many have failed the character test and given up because they couldn't take the hard work. You stayed with it don't give up!

Chapter One

Who are you?

In this chapter I will describe some of the people who apply for a tattoo apprenticeship. You need to be honest with yourself and ask yourself why you want to be a tattooist because attitude to the trade and your customers is just as important as outstanding work. You need to produce good work but be humble because if you have a huge ego you will fall as many a good tattooist has found out to their cost.

The total dreamer who has no drawing ability- There are people who just cannot draw. They know they cannot draw but they believe a good tattooist can "teach" them. Tattooists are born to tattoo and are not really taught but more guided on the technical side of tattooing and how to develop their talent. Some people are not sure what they want to do with their life and have watched a few tattoo programmes on TV and have fallen in love with what they perceive the lifestyle of a tattooist to be. They think tattooists get up late after a hard nights partying then go to work when they feel like it, sit around the shop all day playing computer games, take some drugs, do a really cool tattoo take some more drugs and then go home after earning a small fortune. I'm afraid the reality is you will be answering emails and preparing drawings all night for the next days work and then working hard all the next day.

The person who has some talent but is lazy- Despite what some may think tattooing is hard work. Whether you are tattooing a long line of people in a street shop or concentrating real hard on a photo realistic portrait or trying to make some custom piece work and flow tattooing requires a lot of concentration and can be very tiring. To run a successful shop with a good reliable reputation you need to produce good work daily – and these days with a smile. So there is no room for laziness, incidentally if you are the "arty farty" type and need to be "in the right mood" to produce art or have an ego problem you may still get some work but you won't be able to run a solid business.

Advice for the person who has some talent but is lazy- You have potential but you really need to get your finger out if you are going to make it.

The person who has lots of talent but is lazy- As above but be careful you have lots of talent but someone with less talent than you but more enthusiasm could overtake you.

The person who has lots of talent and lots of enthusiasm- This book was wrote for you. World champions are made from people who are born with exceptional talent and then they push it as far as they can go.

Advice for the person with lots of talent and lots of drive- You will make it. Please follow my advice later on in the book, if you follow my advice I am sure you will get a job somewhere just don't give up.

Advice for the general reader- Ask yourself honestly which of the above categories do you fall into. I cannot stress enough if you have no drawing ability this book is not for you neither is a career in tattooing but if you have outstanding ability the techniques described later in the book will at best get you a job offer on the spot or at worst it will be the best advice you are going to get from a tattooist.

Chapter Two

How not to apply

I know you haven't bought this book to learn how not to apply but it is just as important to know what not to say or do when applying for a tattoo apprenticeship. Here's a good starting point be very careful what you put online or on social networking sites it might sound obvious but you will be surprised the amount of people that post negative stuff online that will go against them for applying for any job. For a shop owner employing new staff it's not just about the artwork the applicants attitude is just as important, its no good having the best artist in the world working in your shop if they have a bad attitude are arrogant, have a huge ego and are addicted to booze and drugs. A shop owner can find these things out about you or at least get a good idea of what you are about by taking a quick look at your Facebook page so good advice is to delete anything that might go against you when applying for a tattoo apprenticeship and then being positive you could post lots of fresh positive stuff that inspires and will help you.

Do not phone tattoo shops asking for an apprenticeship. The shop receptionist will have already been told to tell all wannabes where to go (In fact this could be one of your first jobs when you get your apprenticeship, ironic eh?). Do not turn up at the shop and tell the tattooist you have "been having a go" at home with an ebay kit, trust me this is very offensive to a tattooists ears, you have to be a professional tattooist to truly understand what I mean. Don't ever turn up at a tattoo shop asking for an apprenticeship without a portfolio. Do not bullshit or try and make out you know more about the trade than you really do, to an experienced tattooist it stands out a mile and you really make yourself look stupid for instance people that do this usually refer to parts of our equipment by names we would never use this tells us instantly they haven't got a clue and the fact they are bullshitting really puts us off considering them for any kind of job. All this stuff may seem obvious but evidently it's not otherwise so many people wouldn't do it. I've lost count of the people who say to me "I'm really good at drawing and want to do tattooing" I then reply "Let's see your portfolio then" to which they say " I haven't got one". Your portfolio is everything if you haven't yet got one I suggest you start working on it right away as you will not get offered a job or an apprenticeship without one. What shop owner in their right mind would offer an apprenticeship to someone without having any idea of what they are capable of? This may sound like I am ranting here but I'm describing real life experiences here that may sound negative but we can turn them into a positive by learning from them and avoiding these pitfalls.

If you do already have a portfolio great but work on improving it and making it stronger. Never fake a portfolio to get an apprenticeship otherwise you will end up doing a year's or more apprenticeship cleaning the toilets etc. and when you are finally allowed to do a tattoo you will have spent a year's apprenticeship cleaning toilets all for nothing because believe me when it's obvious you are not capable of doing what's in your portfolio you will be out of the door .

So be very careful out there, remember the golden rule don't pay for an apprenticeship or so called "tattoo college" courses, tattoo shop owners aren't the slightest bit interested in fake tattoo school certificates only good solid strong portfolios.

Chapter Three

Avoid being ripped off

When you ask an established tattooist for an apprenticeship ask yourself what you have to gain. You have everything to gain and nothing to lose. Now ask yourself what an established tattooist has to gain by taking you on as an apprentice. He could teach you everything he knows, pass on his very hard earned wisdom only for you to open your own shop very close by in direct competition taking half of the shops clients with you. So you see you have everything to gain while the tattooist has everything to lose. Wannabes don't seem to think this through and wonder why their local tattooist doesn't welcome them with open arms.

A good quality apprenticeship is worth many thousands of pounds. Unfortunately most people don't have this sort of money at their disposal so the traditional way of paying this is to work it off, hence cleaning toilets for a year or more without pay.

There are two longstanding apprenticeship rip offs in the industry.

The first one consists of taking as much money as possible from you as a "fee" for your apprenticeship and then teach you nothing or very little that you couldn't pick up yourself from watching online videos. Maybe there are people out there who are successful tattooists who did pay for there apprenticeship but I would say be very careful of handing over large sums of money especially if you are a dreamer and can't draw, you will be asking to get ripped off.

I know of a tattooist who when he is asked the question "Do you take on apprentices?" he replies "Yes I do, it's nine hundred pounds a week and you can start next Monday". When the wannabe nearly faints with excitement the tattooist says "Oh yeah I forgot to mention I don't accept cheques", meaning you have to pay him nine hundred pounds a week!

The second rip off is to make you work as a dogsbody for the dogsbody part of your apprenticeship with the shop benefitting from free labour with no intention of teaching you anything. I have heard horror stories where the tattooist really abuses you like punches or kicks you when he's in a bad mood (or even in a good mood), and then when you turn up with a new girlfriend as far as he's concerned she's his!

Don't get me wrong here if you are in a genuine quality apprenticeship it is priceless and you should be the shops dogsbody while you are paying it off.

Chapter Four

Portfolio is everything

When you apply for a job as a tattooist or an apprenticeship your portfolio is what "sells" you, along with your personality, attitude and appearance.

Therefore you need a portfolio as strong as possible. If you have already done a bit of tattooing you should make sure you photo everything and get as much varied portfolio as possible. If you have never tattooed you need an even stronger portfolio of drawings. Other artistic projects help, if you have done painting, airbrushing or even unrelated art like sculpture or pottery put it in your portfolio it will show you are a true all round artist. Again your drawings should be as varied as possible showing you can work in all styles. Try and put as much original art in your portfolio as possible we can all copy standard flash otherwise we wouldn't be tattooists. The tattoo industry is so saturated now everybody's looking for the next big thing which is always original art. If your artwork is mediocre you will not make it as the industry is overcrowded with good artists!

Now assuming you have a good quality portfolio the next thing to do is put it online. You don't need your own website although of course this will make you look more serious, keen and professional, a social network site will do, it's the portfolio that really counts, the best website with a mediocre portfolio will not get you a job but an exceptional portfolio on a social network page will. Now your portfolio is online it will be easier to show busy potential shop owners your portfolio at their leisure with the added bonus that they could show it to their colleagues that may be looking for a new artist if they think your work is good but they don't have a position available for you.

Chapter Five

How to present your work and approach tattooists

So now you have an outstanding portfolio and you are ready to show it to shop owners hoping to get a tattooing apprenticeship.

The very first thing you should do is research the shop you are going to pitch to. Have a really good look at their website to see what they are about. I can tell who has or has not researched me because some people ask me questions that are clearly answered on my website, or worse still they do things that I ask them on my website not to do like show me tiny bits of artwork on their mobile phones instead of presenting it the correct way on paper.

I know when you are keen to get an apprenticeship you will accept any shop that will take you but if your portfolio is truly outstanding trust me you have more choice than you think. You don't really want to work in a place that has a bad atmosphere or too many egos. Just like you wouldn't let a tattooist tattoo you if he didn't have a portfolio don't pitch to a shop that hasn't got a website remember the rogues that are out to rip you off. Of course not all shops that haven't got a website are disreputable but you can't look at their website to make your own mind up can you?

Try and avoid shops that have been opened by the apprentice of an established shop who has fallen out with the boss and opened his own shop too early before he is qualified, by qualified I mean he is not competent and still doing scratchy work. There are many pitfalls to working in a shop like this. Firstly if the guy has fallen out with people the chances are he will fall out with you, secondly a lot of these shops don't last because the boss falls out with people, he is too arrogant to finish his apprenticeship therefore he is doing sub standard work but selling it as professional standard thereby building a very bad reputation for the shop and thirdly he has no experience of running a shop. Around the year 2000 these types of shop were opening everywhere they were like a cancer with apprentices opening their own shop within a very short space of time and then taking on yet more apprentices, it was like the blind leading the blind, these types of shop earn the worst reputation believe me you do not want to be working in one picking up all sorts of bad habits.

From the shops website you obviously need to find out who the chief hirer and firer is, it's no good giving the best pitch in the world to the tea boy who has no authority to give you a job. If you ask anybody but the boss they might decide for the boss that the shop doesn't need another tattooist and send you on your way.

The second thing to research from the shops website after you have found out who the boss is, is to look at the shops portfolio to see what kind of work they do. Choose shops that do the kind of work you are interested in and like doing as your first choice of shop to work in. If you can't find the type of shop that does the work you like to do as an alternative you could point out the benefits of taking on an extra artist who specialises.

Approaching tattooists today is much easier than it used to be when I started tattooing. If you walked in to a tattoo shop in the nineteen seventies and said you were interested in becoming a tattooist at best they would completely ignore you as if you were not there and did not exist, at worst they would physically throw you out of the shop and if there were any stairs involved there would be a very high chance that you wouldn't be going back down them by the traditional method of using your feet.

Today's tattooists are much more friendlier due to the huge amount of tattoo shops there now are.

So now you have an outstanding portfolio, you have done your research and you are ready to pitch to the tattoo shop of your first choice. Now here is the great secret, confidently approach the boss, do not ask for an apprenticeship, it is very important that you don't mention the words apprenticeship or apprentice at any time, then politely ask him if he would mind looking at your portfolio (insinuating that you would like him to point you in the right direction of improving it). Now you will find out how good your portfolio really is. Trust me if your portfolio is truly outstanding, you are the real deal and the shop owner is the real deal, if he needs somebody he will offer you an apprenticeship/job on the spot. If he doesn't it can only mean one of two things, either your portfolio wasn't as good as you thought it was or he simply does not have a vacancy at the moment.

If it's the latter obviously don't give up. If your portfolio is good enough and you present it exactly as I have described somebody somewhere will definitely give you a job if they have the space for another artist, no doubt about it. I would recommend you physically go around all the tattoo shops as I have described but if you are going to send your portfolio by email unsolicited one piece of good advice I would give you is to include a photo of yourself. Sometimes I receive such emails and I think to myself I wonder if this person has toilet roll holes through their ears, tusks through their nose, and tattoos all over their face, this would put off customers in some shops but would encourage customers in others. Being heavily tattooed I know full well people shouldn't judge you by your appearance but I'm afraid human nature being what it is people most definitely do. Most bosses don't care what the hell your appearance is but they do care what their customers think, and if they think your appearance is going to lose or gain trade they will accept or refuse you accordingly. Another very good piece of advice is, is to get some business cards made up with a nice photo on it of your best work and contact details linked to your website, to your portfolio and to yourself, then after presenting yourself to a shop owner exactly as I have described you get turned down politely ask if you may leave them your card. I have on occasion been impressed with somebody's portfolio but have been busy and for one reason or another turned them away and regretted it later only to wish I had remembered to ask them to leave their contact details, being on the receiving end don't let a shop owner forget you leave them your card, contact details and a reminder of the quality work in your portfolio. Good Luck!

Chapter Six

Summary

To summarise remember the techniques in this book will not work if you cannot draw. If you have outstanding ability and have built a strong varied portfolio they most definitely will. Remember to never ask for an apprenticeship outright as the answer will usually be a no. Present your portfolio in front of the shop owner. Never give up. Keep trying different shops time and time again using the same technique. Always leave your contact details so if the shop owner changes his mind or has a vacancy later in the future he can contact you. Have faith in the technique as I know if I wanted more staff and they presented themselves and their work exactly as I have described as long as their portfolio was truly outstanding and I liked their appearance I wouldn't hesitate to hire them , I also know I have many friends and colleagues who would also prefer to be approached this way rather than the usual wannabe making a nuisance phone call.

When you do finally make it as a fully qualified tattooist respect the old school ways and work with integrity.

If one day you open your own shop be your own man (or woman), open in a new area and don't try and steal the hard work somebody else has built up. Trust me if you find your own pitch you will have more trade and you will build up a much more solid clientele in the long run.

When I started tattooing tattooists had a lot more respect for each other, now a newcomer will not think twice about opening very close using the excuse "tattooists are everywhere, wherever I open it will be close to somebody". This is complete bullshit. A friend of mine worked in my shop for over ten years when the time was right for him to open his own shop he found an empty town fifteen miles away. This is the correct way of doing things he is a true tattooist in every way. Others opened within two miles of me before he opened his shop. Because he did the right thing I know for a fact his shop is much busier than theirs and he has had less time to build the trade. I often drive through places that have no tattoo shop and I am not looking for an empty pitch!

Finally I wish you the very best of luck, I hope the advice in this book has been of some use to you, where I have appeared to rant or be negative this was only telling it as it really is and aimed at people that don't really want to be tattooists but just think the lifestyle is cool to true future tattooists such as yourself you will see all of it as positive and I sincerely wish you the best of luck and hope you fit in somewhere whether it be a position in an established shop or one day own your own shop. If you do manage to land your dream job by following the techniques in this book I would love to hear from you, drop me a line.

Sean Hobden

©2012

Updated 2020

ABOUT THE AUTHOR

Sean Hobden has been in the tattoo trade for almost 40 years. He rented his first high street shop at the age of twenty one after serving in the army, he then bought a bigger shop at the age of twenty five which he still owns to this day. His shop is now one of the longest established in the South East of England.

www.ingramcontent.com/pod-product-compliance
Lightning Source LLC
Chambersburg PA
CBHW031510210526
45463CB00008B/3173